The Amazing Weight

"The Gift, Grief, Glory and Grace of the Called'

Marissa R. Farrow
© 2018 by Marissa Farrow
Published by Halo Creative Group
A division of Marissa Farrow LLC.
P.O. 35356 Dulaney Valley Rd. Towson, MD 21204
www.MarissaFarrow.com
E-book edition created 2018
ISBN 978-1725086647

This book is written in dedication to a generation that has been set on fire by the weight of glory, called to a great work. May you forever stand – even with the weight!

TABLE OF CONTENTS

FOREWORD

A couple of years ago, I had the privilege of hearing this young daughter of thunder minister at a conference in Ft. Washington. I knew right then that she was on a path to make a Godly impact wherever her gift takes her. I knew the gift that was on her would bring grief and glory. Furthermore, she would have to, like many of us who came before her, carry the weight of gift and assignment—the amazing weight: the gift, grief and glory of the called.

Marissa transparently talks about all three: the gift, the grief and the glory. With insight from the life of David and the life of Jesus to her own personal life, she seeks to come to grasp with living with the gift and the grief of the called. Her transparency is to be admired as well as to be a model to those who have sensed a calling on their lives, but also live between the grief and the glory. I know about the amazing weight, being in ministry for over 20 years.

In Marissa's book you will find the glory outweighs the grief and you will find practical, powerful lessons to apply to your life with the amazing weight of ministry and mission.

Most importantly you will find reassurance that faithful is He who called you, who also will do it. 1 Thessalonians 5:24

Dr. Jasmin Sculark
Senior Pastor
Victory Grace Center
& CEO of Dr. Jazz Ministries
Bowie, MD

INTRODUCTION

(The Duality of the call)

All of my life I was told that I was called to be something. However, at that time, I couldn't identify with the extent of that call. However, I was told that what I was called for wouldn't be easy. That the journey would be long, hard, and I would have many days when I walked alone. At fourteen years old, I had no clue what the entirety of this all meant. I remember developing in ministry – not particularly my preaching ministry, but serving in ministry in the church – and even as a young always feeling as if it was complicated. On the one hand you felt a passion, but on the other you felt the pressure of serving. I never quite understood how the thing we are supposed to do could sometimes be the thing that becomes a point of conflict for us. Consider the biblical prophet Jeremiah. He had a great gift from God, the ability to foretell and speak the word of God through the gift of prophecy, but he was known as the "lamenting" or "weeping" prophet, for it was that same special calling that grieved him at times. Gifts are special. They are beautiful and they are Godly, but what happens when the gift causes you grief? When it's too heavy to bear? When you are required to maintain your posture through the pressure your gift brings? When you are carrying something that is amazing and heavy? Honorable but hard? Beautiful but burdensome? It's *The Amazing Weight*.

But he that knew not, and did things worthy of stripes, shall be beaten with few stripes. And to whomsoever much is given, of him shall much be required: and to whom they commit much, of him will they ask the more. - Luke 12:48 ASV

I remember the day I discovered and identified this internal war. I remember feeling like there is always this pervasive pull on my life that causes me to experience a duality of emotions. Duality, meaning there were two very strong feelings existing in one mental and emotional space. If you had asked me, I would have said it was abnormal because similarly to love and hate being incapable of existing in the same space, I didn't quite get how the duality of my emotions could reside in the same space. But then I realized my mother, and probably every mother on the face of this planet has at some point felt this way. So, there I was at the Four Seasons spa, laying in the relaxation room looking intently into the perfectly placed lights. Head back, body still, mind racing. For months I had been feeling caught between transition. I didn't quite know the details of what was before me. I just knew options were swarming over my head – and at some point, one would stop in front of me as a door of opportunity that I was destined to walk through. Then here comes this moment where it seems like a door had closed and life was happening fast. I was receiving calls I had never received, going places I had never been, meeting people I had never met, walking in rooms I had never imagined, and it was all good. For a moment, it finally felt as if one of those swarming doors had stopped in front of me, and it was my moment to walk in and embrace it. I felt settled and it seemed like I had a clear view of how the next 3-5 years of my life would look. So, I'm staring into this light and a smile hits my face. Almost like a sigh of relief as to say,

"Finally, I feel steady". I'm thinking of all the great things that could possibly come from this window of destiny and the smile was soon accompanied with tears that began to stream down my face. The longer I looked, the faster and harder the tears came. And that's when I thought for one moment, maybe I am emotionally unstable! I even began to reason with myself by saying "Marissa, for the first time in months you feel sure about what's happening around you. Why are you crying?" My answer was hard to come to grips with. Let's be clear: I tell everyone there are two people you should never lie to, and they are the two people who know you best, you and God. So, I couldn't deny my reality, I was READY, but I was also reserved. Because I realized that with this gift comes grief. That's when I discovered *The Amazing Weight*. Something so heavy and so glorious, something so painful but so rewarding, something so weighty but so necessary, something that makes you laugh and makes you cry, something that is your rain yet also your umbrella – the thing you can't stop chasing, but the thing you may want to stop running after. There's such a beautiful whirlwind that comes with this gift. I wasn't alone though remember? Every mother at

Marissa Farrow   10

some point has experienced an amazing weight. Because for nine months they carry this gift in their wombs, and it has to be a gift because only God can give life. But after that nine-month period, there is a burden that is attached to birthing that gift because that gift doesn't come without the pain of the push. If not the push, then the cut – the chaos, the turmoil, the trauma – and sometimes even the critical moment determining if that gift lives or dies. But while every mother loathes the pain of the push, the tears that they cry when the gift is released are tears that are full of the duality of the call to mother this gift because there's such a pain but such a purpose that exists in one space. These are not just tears of joy but also of relief – relief in knowing that the moments that required a push for the gift to come out were necessary. And for this, mothers are consumed with a beautiful pain because they know that although the pain was great, it was worth it. Furthermore, the dichotomy of this call would not only exist in the push of delivery but in the press to keep nurturing and growing this gift with all the challenges that comes along with it. The pain of pushing but the joy of birthing is an amazing weight. It's the same contrast that exists within those who are called to anything because there is no birthing of gifts, no pushing of preparation and promotion without the duality of the call.

There cannot be a separation. However, just because two conflicting emotions are existing in one space doesn't mean the gift is rejected or regretted. I can assuredly say that the weight wasn't one that made me regret my call. That while there are times when it may be heavy on me, it won't stop calling me. I couldn't stop running after it, I couldn't stop the joy of it, and I was happy about the results of it. So why the weight? What is the weight? The weight is the other side of the dichotic relationship. It's the opposite of the joy, and that's the grief. What is grief exactly? Good question. Grief is deep sorrow, not limited to being caused by a death. Sorrow being a deep distress, so it's not necessarily a regret. This grief is not mourning. It is intense distress, and distress is certainly a part of the duality of this call. It's not a sin to be distressed. In fact, there were great people in the Bible who experienced *The Amazing Weight*. Two people stand out whose journeys have helped me to manage my own amazing weights. One is King David. Biblically, he is referenced as one of the greatest kings to ever reign over Israel. So much of the Bible covers in his life in great detail and chronicles his journey as a boy, warrior, man, and king. It shows us in great extent the cost of being the called. How glorious and difficult the same call can be. But what about Jesus? Savior of the entire world. He experienced an amazing weight! It was called Calvary. The entire experience: the garden, the courts, the beating, the walk, and the cross. He expressed its gravity from the beginning, for He prays a prayer to His father, "Father if it is possible, may this cup be taken from me, yet not as I will but as you will" – Matthew 26:39 (NIV). The weight of the call is unavoidable. It is not something you can outrun, but it is something you can outlive because with this weight comes grace, the grace you need to get through it! Grace is unexplainable and unmerited. It's something we haven't earned, but something God freely gives. Grace is what covers you in bearing that weight. Grace is what God gives you to go through what you cannot go around. It's the bridge that stands between where you are and where you're going, between what you have and what you need.

Grace is how you can live amidst this weight. There is grace in being called. And when God calls you, He calls you with intention and desire to utilize you as a part of the work and completion of His perfect will. When He calls you, He provides grace for you to stand. If there was no grace, there could be no call because God calls imperfect people to a most Holy and sacred work. There must be grace to use imperfection to fulfill perfect work.

There's grace that covers our flaws, faults, and failures – there's even grace to help us through our hurt, hardships, and heartbreaks. Grace that keeps calling us when we are tired, grace that keeps us motivated when people don't understand or appreciate the work. There's grace to carry you through *The Amazing Weight*.

CHAPTER 1

Amazing Grace

(*Grace for the Weight*)
I Samuel 15

When I was a little girl, I studied my dad avidly and as much of a theological orator as he can be, he wasn't void of wisdom and truth. You're practically always in church when you grow up as a "PK". So many days I watched my dad "introduce the speaker" or preacher for that ministry moment, and out of the plethora of amazing ways my fascinating father could introduce a preacher, my all-time favorite is one that I'll refer to for this reading as the "God's always got somebody" introduction. Whenever my dad would use this introduction, I would always try to record his seamlessly flowing words in my mind, and for what I can piece together now it would go something like this:

"God's always got somebody! When there was a world void without light and life God called Adam; God's always got somebody. When God needed an aid because it wasn't good for man to be alone, God called and created Eve from the rib of that man; God's always got somebody. There was once a people who were trapped under the rule of a pharaoh without grace and through the streams of the Nile in the house of that same ruler God raised up Moses to one day tell Pharaoh to 'let my people go!'; God's always got somebody. There came a time when Israel needed a leader and God raised up a fifteen year old giant slayer named David; God's always got somebody."

My dad could take us all the way to the need for a savior named Jesus Christ and end with "and tonight, God's got somebody". It was the greatest thing I had ever heard although I had heard it time and time again. But the wisdom was found in the truth that every time God needed somebody for a task, a tragedy, and or even a time, He always had somebody. The Bible tells this amazing story

Marissa Farrow   16

about a God who loved humanity so much so that His perfect plan for them has to be fulfilled – and no matter the void, He always had somebody. Where there is a need to complete the plan, God will raise up one who is capable of handling the call. Here comes the need for David, as well as God's grace for the weight of the call on his life.

The fifteenth chapter of First Samuel records the account of the fall of King Saul, a man who was called to be king over Israel but whose ambition and disobedience caused him to be rejected by God. This story outlines the grace created for David to stand where Saul had failed. In the Old Testament scripture, there was always a call and fulfillment of 3 primary offices: the priest, the prophet, and the king. Samuel was the prophet during the reign of Saul and was the one who anointed Saul for the position of kingship, while Eli was the priest who taught Samuel. Here we see these three major Old Testament offices being filled – priest, prophet, and king. The chapter opens with Samuel telling Saul he anointed Saul as king solely based on his office as prophet after receiving a direct order from the Lord. In this moment, Samuel is emphasizing to

Saul that the directions that were to come are from the Lord. He says "...listen now to the message from the Lord" (NIV), followed by specific instructions to go and attack the Amalekites and spare nothing. During this dispensation of The Law, we witness the wrath of a "terrible God". The instructions were to spare nothing, including children, cattle, and women; spare nothing! But the first thing Saul does during the ambush according to verse nine is spare Agag and the best of the sheep, cattle, fat calves, and lambs. They spared everything that was good to them, but that the Lord gave instruction to destroy. But anything that was despised and weak, they destroyed. Let's put a post-it right here to notate that whenever God gives you instructions, it is important to follow the extent of them ever if and when it doesn't make sense. Sometimes what looks good to us, isn't good to God or according to the plan of God. The problem with Saul was that he was unable to keep God's instruction because he was focused on what seemed good to him. In these times, cattle and livestock were a sign of worth and wealth – the more you had, the wealthier you were. We cannot become so caught up in the wealth of the world that we ignore the instructions of God. Saul wanted to maintain these things for his house and his people but what he was accepting into his life was displeasing in the eyes of God. We must get to a place where we become uncomfortable with bringing things in our space that displease God. When we bring things that are displeasing to God into our space, we allow it room to contaminate other areas of our lives. Saul wanted to keep what appeared good to him of the livestock – which was the same livestock that was used to offer up burnt offerings to God as a sign of worship and atonement – but he was trying to maintain what God was displeased with. We must think critically here: not only did they get rid of what looked weak because they could not live on or consume weak livestock, but burnt offerings were required to be "clean" and "perfect". And although they were instructed by God to destroy it all, Saul and the others kept the livestock that would have been sufficient for burnt offerings – a sign of worship that looked good to them but was contaminated in the eyes of God. We must be careful with what we present to God because what is good to us may be contaminated to Him. You cannot expect God to be pleased with contaminated worship.

You cannot expect God to bless what He has told you to get rid of. This includes friendships, relationships, habits, and ways that we want God to accept that are not pleasing to Him.

As a result of Saul's decisions, according to verse ten of this chapter, the Lord came to Samuel and said "I regret making Saul king."

And here is the grace for David. God's plan must and will be fulfilled regardless of the characters used to fulfill it. This is why obedience to God is not only important but merited because God can use anybody, and where there is a need for God's perfect will to be fulfilled there is a measure of grace for the called to fulfill it. The bible instructs us that "…to each one of us grace has been given as Christ apportioned it." – Ephesians 4:7 (NIV). Christ has allocated a measure of grace to each of us as He has deemed necessary. When there is a placement in the earth that God desires for you to fulfill, He will grace you for your assignment. With grace comes a divine covering or contract between God and those whom He has called which allows room for growth within that call. Grace is not only there to protect us from ourselves and our wrong, grace is there to bridge the gap between what we have and what we need. God calls imperfect individuals to inspirational assignments that work towards the accomplishment of God's perfect will. The understanding of those imperfections requires grace and we live in the dispensation of grace. The shedding of Jesus' blood provides grace for our assignment despite the shortcomings of our humanity. Additionally, when you have grace for the weight of your assignment, you essentially have a safety net that gives you an allotment of understanding and compassion from Christ for the weight of what you carry because while it is difficult, it is necessary.

David was called to stand where Saul had failed. There was a grace for him because there was a need for him. Not that God has to choose or use us, but God desires to use us. There was a need for one whose heart and obedience could be trusted by God. David is described as being a "Man after God's own heart", but that didn't nullify the fact that David was also a liar, a murderer, an adulterer, and a conspirator; however, there was grace for him amidst his faults and failures as a man. Often the weight of our call comes from the pressure we feel to be perfect. This pressure is not only felt from people but it is pressure that we place on ourselves. We know the sacredness of the call on our lives but we also understand the fight against our humanity. So why are we called? Knowing we will fail God? The answer is simply because Christ has come to give us grace to operate where there is a need in the earth. The world is full of imperfect people, imperfect places, and imperfect opportunities. It is not easy to live a life where the pull of perfection fights against the nature of your flesh, but there is grace for you because there is need for you. With that understanding we must be able to properly identify our ability within our call. It is not that we aren't to strive for perfection, but we must know that when we fall there is grace to help us recover in Christ as long as we seek God with earnest repentance. The weight of the call can weigh on you so heavily until you reach a place of disillusionment regarding your ability. Too often we see people buckle under the pressure of this call because they put more on themselves than what is truly possible. God is not void of knowledge about our short comings. Short comings not always equivalent to sin. Sometimes those short comings have to simply do with our needs to be accepted, acknowledged, and loved; our desires to be liked, honored, and cherished; and our desires to be received, etc. Sometimes those short comings deal with our need to never experience some of the feelings we have experienced in our pasts such as rejection, abandonment, and the other things that cause us to live out of our emotions and the moments we experience in our humanity. These things play a great part on the weight of the call because you desire to excel in what you are called to be and you do not want to feel like you've failed or let down the God you've been called by. You operate knowing that it is an honor to be called and not only that, but knowing that people depend on you to fulfill that call. It is a weight knowing other people depend on you when sometimes you simply need to be the one to depend on others. That is why it is important to have a support system that understands the weight of the assignment. David's grace was found in the necessity for his life. There is a need for you – without such, there wouldn't have been a call. You have grace for the call on your life. Walk in that grace, as it is the only thing that can help you to carry the weight.

Grace is the free and unmerited favor of God as manifested in the salvation of sinners and the bestowing on of blessings. Some of us struggle to walk in our grace because we attach it to our personal thoughts about our deservingness of it. But grace from God is unmerited, unwarranted, unjustified. There is no explanation of the grace given to us, it is simply given as Christ has died for it and for us. Because God is omniscient in thought, grace was purchased with the power of the blood – knowing He would use ordinary people to complete an extraordinary work, knowing that we would need a solution to help us to stand. Grace is unexplainable. It is a part of the nature of God that we may never understand. However we don't have to be able to understand why there is grace to receive grace! We must be able to accept what we can't explain because trying to figure it out can diminish our liberty in walking in and accepting grace. But scripture has given us the lead way to walk in that grace; "Stand fast therefore in the liberty wherewith Christ hath made you free. And be not entangled again with the yoke of bondage." – Galatians 5:1(KJV).

As I visit the close of this chapter, I am reminded of how the hymnal lyrics of *Amazing Grace* speaks to the theology of grace. There is no explanation for it, only the presence of it.

Amazing grace how sweet the sound that saved a wretch like me, I once was lost but now I'm found t'was blind but now I see. – John Newton

There is no explanation between the issue and the resolution: "I once was lost but now I'm found, t'was blind but now I see." This is how grace works. There is no blueprint for the compensation it gives. Grace is the bridge that stands between what we lack and what we need. It is freely given to us to help us stand in this perfect work as imperfect people.

CHAPTER 2

Anointed For the Assignment

(The Gift)

I Samuel 16

The act of anointing dates back to early Old Testament scripture. The anointing in early scripture was used for everything – from healing to a sign of honor given as gifts. In its official capacity, it was a rite of inauguration when officials were being appointed to the offices of priest, prophet, or king. It was an act of preparing them for their office, as they were expected to carry out that which was sacred in the way of their humanity. In Old Testament scripture, humanity was under the dispensation of the law and so those who were placed in high offices had to be anointed or purified and sanctified for these positions. Throughout time, we have seen people who were anointed or set apart for God's work, and to the same degree it is a reverent act that is designed to symbolically and publically set apart what has already been called by God. This is similar to what we see in the modern church where we use Holy oils to anoint individuals – not as a sign that there is any power in the oil as much as there is in the act of being anointed or set apart from the common man or sinners. While this is a defining act in the life of the called, the anointing began in its conception in the mind and plan of God before the beginning of time. This truth is expressed to us with the call of Jeremiah: "Before I formed you in the womb I knew you, before you were born I set you apart; I appointed you as a prophet to the nations." – Jeremiah 1:5 (NIV).

The anointing has always been a method of Christ by which we are called and used. For the sanctification or setting apart of those who are called. But the anointing begins much like what is stated in Jeremiah – before conception. God, in His infinite wisdom, has outlined a plan for the salvation of humanity and He has ordained a role for everyone in it. There is no one who is birthed by incident nor accident, for it is only God who gives life and God never moves without intention. In His plan He has chosen people for different works, but the anointing is within. In the same regard God knows all of our short comings and failures before He calls us. He told Jeremiah "I knew you". The word "knew" indicates a past tense. How then did God already know he who was not yet formed in the womb? Because God's wisdom is simply so, that He knows our ending from our beginning as indicated to us in the word given through the Prophet Isaiah:

Remember the former things of old: for I am God, and there is none else; I am God, and there is none like me, Declaring the end from the beginning, and from ancient times the things that are not yet done, saying, My counsel shall stand, and I will do all my pleasure... – Isaiah 46:9-10 (KJV)

We as Christians must get to the point where we wholeheartedly and assuredly understand this concept of knowing who God is. Until we understand the nature of God to man we won't fully accept how He sees us and His heart toward us. God is personal: He is one we can interact with. God is compassionate: He is one who cares. God is loving: He feels for humanity. When we understand God's nature, we will relieve ourselves of some of the struggle that comes with trying to balance ourselves between a spiritual call in a human form.

The literal anointing comes prior to the act of anointing. Therefore, what we see and believe to be the act of the anointing is simply a public confirmation of that which has already been privately, personally, or inwardly revealed.

In I Samuel 16, we witness the anointing of David who we know has been called by God before time but has been given grace to stand where Saul has failed. David was not perfect but yielded. The Lord speaks to Samuel and asks him how long he will mourn over Him having rejected Saul as king over Israel. Then He gives Samuel the instructions to "Fill your horn with oil and be on your way; I am sending you to Jesse of Bethlehem. I have chosen one of his sons to be king." – 1 Samuel 16:1 (NIV). So Samuel goes down to the house of Jesse and when he arrived, he saw one of Jesse's sons by the name of Eliab. Because of his appearance, Samuel thought that he was the one that the Lord had anointed but the Lord then told him in verse seven:

... Do not consider his appearance or his height, for I have rejected him. The Lord does not look at the things people look at. People look at the outward appearance, but the Lord looks at the heart. – I Samuel 16:7 (NIV)

This is a pivotal understanding in the life of the called. The anointing and call by God is not contingent upon any particular circumstance but is done simply by the decision of God. There is no set of credentials that qualifies anyone for the calling and in the same regard there is no set of inadequacies that disqualifies you for the call – because man looks at the outward appearance but God looks at the heart. Degrees won't validate it, affirmations won't change it, and agreements won't make it any stronger. Those things can mature what already exist but it will not add or take away from the anointing. An alcoholic can be called, a homeless person can have a call. There is no system that qualifies nor disqualifies your anointing. Anointing is like matter, it cannot be created nor destroyed. It is simply existent and innate within us as given to us by God before the beginning of time, conceived within the limitlessness of God's mind.

Some of us will better reason with the weight of what we carry when we realize that while there is a standard we live up to, God "KNEW" us in and out before He called us.

So Samuel goes forth – son by son – looking for the one God has anointed for kingship. Seven sons in total passed him, but none of them were the one. That's how the anointing is, either you have it or you don't. There is really no in-between for YOUR assignment. With this, it is imperative to know your call. Every one isn't anointed for every assignment, but your anointing will stand strong, unwavering, and unquestioned for YOUR assignment. Samuel examined all seven sons and none of them were the chosen one for this particular assignment. This in no way indicted that there wasn't an assignment in which they were called for, but kingship wasn't it. Samuel now asks Jesse in verse ten of this chapter; "are these all the sons you have?" And Jesse replies, "There is still the youngest…he is tending to the sheep." They send for David and when he arrives the scriptures say that he was glowing with health and had a fine appearance and handsome features, but even those characteristics were rejected in Eliab. The next verse is what brings clarity to how we know that David was the chosen one. Verse twelve says:

Then the Lord said rise and anoint him; this is the one. So Samuel took the horn of oil and anointed him in the presence of his brothers, and from that fay on the spirt of the Lord came powerfully upon David. Samuel then went to Ramah. – I Samuel 16:12-13 (NIV)

It's important to notate that the act of the anointing was a public affirmation of what was already formulated in the plan and mind of God. The above scripture states that the spirit of the Lord came powerfully upon David from that day. The act of the anointing provided a direction for that which was at work in David.

The anointing of God cannot be given or taken away by any man. When the pressure of the call begins to weigh you down, you must be mindful of from whom your anointing comes: the God who "knew" you and who knows every part of you. God is personal and acclimated with every fiber of our being as His children. While He is personal, compassionate, and loving, He is also a Father. He loves us as His children:

For ye have not received the spirit of bondage again to fear; but ye have received the Spirit of adoption, whereby we cry, Abba, Father. – Romans 8:15 (KJV)

He is a father, one who is concerned about His children. Often in life the weight that we carry deals with the expectations, and evaluations of people who are not as well acquainted with us as the Father who called us. Sometimes we put so much into spiritual fathers and leaders that shape our thoughts on who we are and who we are called to be. But we must remember that our anointing comes from our Eternal Father. In earthy relationships, our fathers will chastise us, correct us, or even show compassion on us – sometimes differently from other siblings, if we have them, solely based on what they know about us as their children. There are different needs and requirements for each child. We must be acquainted with our father as He is acquainted with us. When you are in relationship, you realize that sometimes you have to control the entrance of outside voices, opinions and evaluations in order to be in touch and in tune with who you are in relationship with. If you fail to manage the noise, you run the risk of ruining the flow of your relationship because you'll find yourself acting according to what is coming from the outside and missing the intent of the one you share with. Excess noise will make the weight of the call heavier. There are some people who are not capable of helping us carry the weight, but our Father who loves us and who cares will never see us with more than we can handle. His word gives us this blessed assurance in these words:

Come unto me, all ye that labour and are heavy laden,
and I will give you rest.

Take my yoke upon you, and learn of me; for I am meek
and lowly in heart: and ye shall find rest unto your souls.
For my yoke is easy, and my burden is light. – Matthew
11:28-30 (NIV)

There is no way around the weight of the anointing.
Carrying the anointing is never an easy task, as it brings
about great requirement and responsibility. However, the
God who has anointed you for the assignment and knew
you before the assignment is capable of helping you to
carry what you are called for. He has given you a grace
for the weight.

CHAPTER 3

After the Anointing

(The Giants Keep Rolling)

I Samuel 17

One thing we learn from David is what life can extensively be like after the anointing. David was anointed to be the future king of Israel between the ages of ten and fifteen. He became king at thirty years old and reigned for forty years. But after he was anointed, there was a process that proceeded the reign. He didn't immediately walk into kingship. And it was after he was anointed that he faced the Philistine giant, Goliath. In this examination of I Samuel 17, we learn a lot from the life of David after the anointing. To begin, we learn that David is not moved by time and pressure. Often we add to the weight of what is naturally beautiful and burdensome in our lives such as our call, allowing ourselves to feel like there is some timeline that is within our control to make it work. All things happen in the time that God allows when he has anointed you. David was anointed by Samuel to be King, but when we find him in this chapter, we find him still shepherding. Think it no coincidence that David is holding a position that to some may seem lowly of a king but is preparing him to be king. In the early verses of this chapter, we find that there is a champion Philistine named Goliath from Gath, who has come out daily to taunt Israel, challenging them to battle. He told them to choose a man to come fight him but no one would come forward knowing and feeling they weren't capable of competing with the champion of the Philistines. David's brothers were there at the war, but David would go back and forth from Saul – whom he was replacing – to attend to his father's sheep in Bethlehem. One day, David was taking food to his brothers at the war, and the important thing to annotate is in verse twenty:

Early in the morning David let the flock in the care of a shepherd, loaded up and set out, as Jesse had directed.
– I Samuel 17:20 (NIV)

David goes back and forth between Saul and Jesse. He has been anointed to be king, but he was also still shepherding! This means that David did not forsake his responsibilities received from his earthly father while in preparation to be king, which was an assignment received from his Heavenly Father. Some of us end up carrying more than we have to because we believe that an anointing merits a certain timeline. So sometimes we get ahead of God trying to fulfill his call. But you can do the right thing in the wrong time and it still be the wrong thing. David didn't get anointed one day and become king the next. The anointing was the indication to him that there was something inside that needed to be directed and matured; something that needed to be grown and groomed. So he spent time humbly submitted to the process that was involved with growing the gift. Even the anointing has a plan attached to it and it includes a placement that God has for you in all you do and will accomplish. Unfortunately, I have seen too often where people become discouraged and dismayed second guessing the call on their lives because everything doesn't happen like they expect it to – after being anointed. Often God will place you in a position to see if you can humbly submit to the process of obedience. David was anointed for kingship but still carried the role of a shepherd by attending to his father's flock. There is no coincidence in the fact that David's time of preparation was in this role because even in the highest office in the land as a king, he would need the skills of a shepherd. Sometimes, while people and outside expectations puts great pressure on that which is already weighty, we add to that pressure by trying to clock God and clock the stages of our call. I often emphasize that God's sovereignty is not subject to our objectivity. This means that we cannot dictate to God what God is supposed to do with His power. In fact, I wouldn't want to, as or minds are finite compared to God's infinite wisdom. Scripture teaches us in Isaiah 55:8-9 that God's thoughts are not like ours, and neither are His ways. That *"As the heavens are higher than the earth, so are my ways higher than your ways and my thoughts than your thoughts."* God's plans for us exceed our understanding. There are things God deems necessary for us to experience and endure as preparation for the promises that He's given us. If we don't learn to embrace the process, we can abort what is necessary for us to survive and sustain in the promise that He has made to and created for us. David didn't jump right into the blessing of kingship. Imagine the ease of life that would have been immediately felt becoming king right away, versus being a shepherd. Yet he was faithful to the process of shepherding because it was preparing him to be king. It is possible for your anointing to carry you where your character cannot keep you. Some of the weight we bear deals much with living up to the standard of what we have been called to, but if you allow yourself the time to develop in the dark room, you will not come out as damaged film. But here's the weight, the dark room isn't easy. David's dark room put him among the sheep. Some of us won't be among the sheep but sheep-like situations. Things that almost seem beneath our call, but these are things that are humbling enough to create a disposition of humility within us and strong enough to prepare us for how to sustain when we reach the destination. The dark room experience is different for everyone. Maybe your dark room included some rejections, or abandonments, generational curses, bad addictions, or self-esteem issues. Whatever the dark room is, it's not pretty, but the picture is clear when the time of developing is complete. We will alleviate some of the weariness that comes with the weight of development when we allow ourselves to understand that we must yield to whatever the process is, stop trying to make it happen in our time, and allow God to guide us through. This is so that when we get where we are going we don't – well, simply put – blow it! Sometimes we add to the weight that already exists with our call trying to run ahead of God with time. Time has a way of causing everything to work out for you, as according to God's will for your life.

David was still shepherding although he was anointed for the throne. Preparation is key, but so is placement. It was during David's time after the anointing when God allowed him to discover his strengths as a man and as a warrior, but it was because of correct placement that he was able to discover this. This same chapter records the events that transpired as David takes on this giant. In this scripture, we see references to a few key concepts that are important for us to adopt about the process that comes after the anointing. David is heading to the war to take his brothers some food while this Giant is taunting all of Israel and David hears Goliath's defiance of Israel. The men of the war heard it and fled but David felt a righteous indignation towards this "uncircumcised Philistine" who was defying the God of Israel. When you are anointed for a specific assignment, what others run from will activate the anointing in you. David goes to Saul and says "I will go and fight him." While Saul questioned David's ability, David felt his own capability based on what he knew was already inside of him. Saul eventually agrees, but Saul thought that it was befitting to give David his armor to wear. When David put on Saul's armor he realized that he was unable to fight in what he was not used to. People will often try to place you in things that aren't yours, especially when dealing with mentoring and/or succession. Sometimes people operate in a mentality that you are called to the same "fit" as them. In other words, people will often try to make you another version of themselves, but you will not be successful in your anointing until you walk in the grace you have been given for your assignment. Trying to live up to methods or thoughts that people may have for you will often frustrate you and may even cause your failure. David told Saul that he could not go and fight in those garments because he was not used to them. Had David gone to fight Goliath trying to fit Saul's idea of what would make him successful, he would have ultimately failed from being stuck, slow, and probably from stumbling. The call to fight Goliath carried its own level of responsibility without adding the weight of carrying someone else's armor. When we deal with what adds to the weight of the call there are many outside forces that make the weight too heavy to bear. But when you walk solely in the grace that is given to you, success is inevitable. What better way to be successful in your calling than to implicitly trust the plan of the One who called you? We must consistently check our motives against our mission to ensure that we keep in mind who we do this for. While our calling is designed to edify, inspire, and serve people, our ultimate duty is to please and submit ourselves to God and His will. As long as we keep His ideas for us at the forefront of our reasoning, we will be graced to walk through any tribulation that may come with the process of reaching the promised places that God has for us.

David decides that he is capable of fighting the giant and ultimately we know the story ends with David having victory over the giant with only a sling and five smooth stones. David's grace gave him the ability to slay what was bigger than him, but the interesting thing here is that this battle comes after he is anointed for the greatest assignment of his life as a King. Before David becomes king he has to go through the process of being a warrior. The weight of the assignment gets heavier and harder to understand when we fail to reason with why God allows us to go through war to become "kings." With the natural weight that comes with being called, we add to the weight by neglecting what could be God's reasoning. Such as the moments in life where we believe God is supposed to prevent calamity on our behalves, when the bible has already explained to us that we will have trouble. Jesus outlines it clearly in John 16:33 (NIV):

I have told you these things, so that in me you may have peace. In this world you will have trouble. But take heart! I have overcome the world.

There are few things in life that are guaranteed but trouble is one of them. We make the already beautifully burdensome road much harder when we have misguided beliefs about life and God in our lives. God designed it so that David would face Goliath. He battled a giant after being anointed.

"Your anointing doesn't exonerate you from experiencing giants."

This is important to understand, for without grasping this you run the risk of further frustrating yourself in the process. Certainly it's not strange that much like David, God has to take us through giants of our own in order to build our confidence in Him, our reputation from others, and the testimony of who we are walking with and who is on our side. Without the giants there is no throne. Those

The Amazing Weight   45

who sit on the throne must know how to battle the giants to maintain the throne. In a more literal sense there is no gain without pain. Sometimes I believe we have a very fairytale idea of God and to have this mindset honestly minimizes the greatness of His majesty. We tend to think that God is some magical being just waiting to make everything perfect in our lives. But truthfully speaking, life isn't designed to be perfect – yet perfecting. We are perfected in the trial, for there is no throne that comes without war. No amount of progress comes without sacrifice and process, and God's wisdom has designed it so that we are able to learn in and grow from our trials.

After you have suffered for a little while, the God of all grace [who imparts His blessing and favor], who called you to His own eternal glory in Christ, will Himself complete, confirm, strengthen, and establish you [making you what you ought to be]. – I Peter 5:10
(AMP)

Trials are designed to prep you. The lesson of this story from David is simple: the giants will keep coming. That is not a sign of a lack of covering by God. Giants come as trials, tribulations, disappointments, and difficulty but these things come to make us strong according to James 1:3. And because God's thoughts for us supersede anything we can ever think or imagine for ourselves, we don't always understand it yet and still we are encouraged in scripture

...that all things work together for good to those who love God, to those who are the called according to His purpose. – Romans 8:28 (KJV)

If we are intimidated by the presence of giants, we make the weight we bear heavier and we give it power to cause us fear. Giants will come, they aren't designed to break you but to build you. Let's face it, nobody wants to tackle a giant but you can if you know that you have been given the grace to conquer that giant and more, as it is a part of God's strategy for your ultimate growth. Be mindful that it is all a part of this great call you have been given and just because you face a giant doesn't mean you don't have a calling. You must remember to place the weights you face in the call in proper perspective in order to maintain your confession that no matter what you face God is still sovereign in it and He alone can help you to bear *The Amazing Weight.*

CHAPTER 4

Celebrated and Scorned

(They Won't Make Up Their Minds)
I Samuel 30

We are called to serve. That is the job and the mission. We have a great calling to lead people and to serve people through the usage of the gifts we have been given. While much of our days are spent focusing on edifying believers, our sincere drive must be towards building and encouraging those who do not believe. However, sometimes the unfortunate truth is that we become so bogged down with trying to win the approval of people that we become off focus with our call and we are more focused and moved by the opinions of people than we are the opinion of the God who called us. If we become caught up in what others think, see, and feel about us we will never be okay with ourselves. This is because people are often unsatisfied and sometimes unrealistic in their expectations of those who lead with a call. I have witnessed a great deal of individuals who become so weighed down by the opinions of the people that they lost themselves and the foundation of their calling.

For unto whomsoever much is given, of him shall be much required: and to whom men have committed much, of him they will ask the more. – Luke 12:48 (KJV)

Expectations are to be expected, but knowing your limitations will help you to eliminate some of the stress and fear of letting people down. Sometimes we can live so on the edge in an attempt to be all things to all people. But **you are a limited resource.** You threaten your physical and mental sanity when you stretch yourself thin. Then what happens when you can't successfully be pastor/leader, father/mother, employee/ entrepreneur – all in one? Because you are a limited resource, if you try to be everything to everybody something WILL without question go lacking. Instead of allowing something to go lacking, you can strategize on how to fulfill other areas with the right teams of people. You can also allow others who have been called to those people to focus their ministry and efforts on reaching those individuals. I was once instructed to make a list of three groups of people that I was called to and prioritize those groups of people so that I can successfully reach them all in my lifetime. But the weight is that those same people you sacrifice your personal wants and path for will at some point hurt, disappoint, betray, and talk about you, while belittling your efforts to serve them. The fact is: some people will never make up their minds. People can be with you like the ones who were with Jesus – cry your praise one week and cry for your crucifixion the next. People can be on your side today and against you tomorrow. Often, people will protect their own best interest and only few will understand your heart enough to stay with you through your mistakes.

This is how David was eventually handled by the people he was called to lead. In I Samuel chapter 30, we watch David be celebrated and scorned. Is this not enough to make anyone question themselves, or feel confusion about if it's worth it? It is difficult to feel like you've given up the things you may have wanted for the sake of the call you've been given, only to feel unappreciated by the people you have sacrificed for. People will rarely understand the depth of what you sacrifice to accept your call. Long nights, early mornings, many tears, the stress of trying to make it all work, the desire to actually please the people you're called to, the nights you don't get to indulge in personal time, the money you give that you may not see back when you need it, and so many other things that can qualify as a sacrifice for the sake of the call. But what about your own dreams, goals, and plans that sometimes you must lay aside for the honor of being called and being used by God? Then you do your best to lead and any sight of error leaves you to the subjections, and scrutiny of the same people you sacrificed for. David understands this from his experience in this scripture when he is attempting to be a great leader. First, he doesn't want to be a one who is viewed as a failure so he is working to be a great leader. This is a personal weight. In this passage we find that David makes an error in his leadership and without much thought, it changes the heart of the people who he is leading. While David was away watching another land, the Amalekites came and raided the place they were inhabiting named Ziklag and they took their treasures, burned their land, took captive their wives, children, and people and "carried them off", according to scripture. The men wept loudly until they couldn't weep anymore. The scripture records that David was greatly distressed because they spoke of stoning him and the key victory is found in verse six where it states that "...David encouraged himself in the Lord" – I Samuel 30:6. Despite the discussion of destroying David, he encouraged himself in the Lord. The same people who sang his praises when he was winning, "Saul has slain his thousands, and David his tens of thousands." – I Samuel 18:7 (NIV), they now want to stone him. It's not easy wavering between being celebrated one moment and scorned the next. This sometimes creates feelings of inadequacy when in all actuality people won't make up their minds. That's why you can only bear this weight when you learn to focus on God. David couldn't run on and lead had he put his focus into the people around him. That's why he encouraged himself in the Lord, because when you have your affections set on God you stop expecting people to ever "pay you back" for what you've done for them.

The overarching theme in all of this is that man adds to the weight that was designed to simply build you and not kill you. While life and your calling can be weighty, it is bearable when you keep God in perspective. We have to be clear on our placement with God to know how to continue to lead and yield to our calling – even when we disappoint people and they in turn disappoint us with failing to acknowledge what we have done. David encourages himself in the Lord. Likewise, you can't look to complex people to help you handle that which is already complex. Your calling is dynamic, it's not some static, stationary position. It is dynamic and it is ever changing. But God specializes in stabilizing us. He alone is capable of giving us the courage we need to stand through the complications of leadership relationships. Sometimes the people we are called to serve will hurt us the most. But the test is determining if you, like David, can stand still in your calling and be steadfast regardless of the season. Sometimes they will make judgments about you that they cannot live up to themselves. In other times they will dislike you before having a chance to get to know you.

But your calling is not about being accepted by man, but accepted by God

CHAPTER 5

Anointed with Agitation

(I'm Anointed, but I've Got a Problem)
II Samuel 11

Throughout the life of David, as chronicled in the Bible, we watch him transition from a boy and warrior to a man and king, but having never lost the intuitions of the warrior. There were things David had to face in kingship that he could only have learned as a warrior. But as David ascends into kingship we watch another dynamic of his life unfold and that is his agitation with temptation and even failure.

Agitation: [ag·i·ta·tion, ajə'tāSH(ə)n/] *the action of briskly stirring or disturbing something, especially a liquid.*

There it was, the thing that was constantly stirring up or disturbing the life of this king. Recorded in many events throughout scripture, David – who was anointed and called before time – dealt with the agitation of temptation. Even so, he was not disqualified from his calling as king. He had to learn to live with and from his errors, understanding that he was called in an imperfect state to a perfect work by a perfect God. That is a difficult concept in and of itself. That is, to negotiate within yourself a balance between doing that which is spiritual wrapped up in the carnality of your flesh, and the weight this contrast alone bears is enough to make any man buckle under pressure. David's anointing – just like ours – not only didn't exonerate him from facing trials, but it also didn't exonerate him from experiencing temptation. The weight or pressure of living up to the expectations placed on you are enough. You must live up to the expectations of God, the expectations of the people you're called to serve, the expectations you place on yourself, all while dealing with a nature that without hesitation pulls you towards temptation and the possibility of failure in that temptation. When fighting a nature that pulls you against the standard you know you've been called to there is a consistent war that is present between spirit and flesh, while you, your mind and the tricks of that mental pressure are left to hang in the balance. The unnerving thoughts of the disappointment God must feel when we fail; the conversations, remarks, and commentary from people who once looked to you as a point of great strength and prominence now see you as a mere man just like them; it all it sends you through this mental struggle to live up to the standard placed before you. The struggle is intensified when you realize you've missed the mark. But none of us are exempt from this agitation. And in line with the common theme of this reading, until we properly put in perspective our abilities, we will always take on more than we can bear. Temptations and failures are inevitable. You will be agitated by these things all of your life. It's not the presence of the agitation that diminishes your character, it is the way you manage the agitation and how you recover when you fail to adequately manage the agitation. God's forgiveness is given to us all, the victim and the murderer, the saint and the sinner. Often we tend to forget that Christ came for the "Jew and Gentile". In other words, He came

Marissa Farrow

for the believer and the barbaric. If there's grace and forgiveness for them, why then do we tend to neglect the notion that God's grace and forgiveness is extended to us in whatever state we find ourselves in? I have watched prominent people fall from God's grace publically who have ended their lives over the weight of their failures. Suicide does not have to be the answer. God's grace and forgiveness works for the fallen sinner just as it works for the fallen preacher, deacon, singer, bishop, pope, and many others. Let's face the truth in this 21st century, we have experienced an array of public figures with private demons. For example and unfortunately, many of the members of the Catholic Church have been under severe pressure and scrutiny for a multiplicity of claims that have come out against the Catholic Church. It seems like there's a recurring national headline of the Catholic Church being placed under the public eye for accusations made about their entity. The difficulty is that it's still the universal church and an indictment against one is unfortunately an indictment against all. It is also an indictment against God from those who are non-believers and those who already hold skepticisms about the church as a whole. We have witnessed some of those same people who have fallen from grace end their lives after their public shame. But there is no amount of failure that God's love cannot reach you in or bring you back from. Perhaps one would debate about the nature and foundation of the call, or if they have been called to ministry in the first place, or if the church is setting people up in a career that requires a call without possessing that call. But even still there's grace and forgiveness for those. David is the ultimate example of God's ability to reach us with His grace, love, and forgiveness.

David after having become king of Israel found himself caught in a matrix of sin after having been tempted and failing in that temptation. The bible records the story of David and his steamy affair with Bathsheba that eventually led to lying, manipulation, and even in modern day terms, him becoming a premeditated accessory to murder. As we journey ahead to II Samuel, we enter more thoroughly into the kingship of David. In chapter 11, one evening David was walking around the roof of his palace and from his location could see a beautiful woman bathing whose name was Bathsheba. In short David asks someone to find out about her and they come back to report her name and that she is the daughter of Eliam and wife of Uriah the Hittite. David proceeds to tell his messengers go and get her. Problem number one: David found out that she was a married woman and David still sent someone to get her. **Essentially he invited in what he should have ignored**. Temptation is a very natural part of this walk which brings a weight with it and if we don't make intentional attempts to check ourselves and manage our temptations, we will set ourselves up for failure. You see, God designed it so that we will *cast our cares upon Him for He careth for us.* Again, when we know the nature of God we know what we can carry to God. He is a personal God who is well acquainted with us, our ways our thoughts, our tendencies, and our idiosyncrasies. He knows them all. When temptation comes, it's important to be open and honest with God about it.

Be anxious for nothing, but in everything by prayer and supplication, with thanksgiving, let your requests be made known to God; – Philippians 4:6 (KJV)

You can even confess your temptations to God in prayer and He is capable of helping you with them, especially in the dispensation we live in, the dispensation of grace, where we have the blessings of a savior who not only knows but empathizes with us and feels for us as confirmed to us in the book of Hebrews:

...we do not have a High Priest who cannot sympathize with our weaknesses, but was in all points tempted as we are, yet without sin. 16 Let us therefore come boldly to the throne of grace, that we may obtain mercy and find grace to help in time of need. – Hebrews 4:15-16 (KJV)

God empathizes with us and what we go through, He is capable of understanding us when we are and when we are not being completely honest with Him. If we begin to properly place God's infinite wisdom above ours we will realize there is nothing that we have to hide from God about ourselves. Instead of playing with the fires that will make you collapse under the weight, learn to go to God before you light the flame. David invited Bathsheba in under the awareness that she was another man's wife.

Your invite can incite if you don't control your impulses. But what we must know is that impulses and temptations don't cause us to collapse under the weight, it's our lack of control over them. David invites Bathsheba in and begins a relationship with her, she becomes pregnant and now David who is still king feels a responsibility towards the situation. However, it is not the kind of responsibility that makes him take ownership over his mistakes, confess them, and seek healing, but the kind that caused him to become deeper engulfed in this spiraling matrix. The bible records, in synopsis, that David sets up Bathsheba's husband, brings him to the palace in an attempt to position him to sleep with his wife to make him believe the baby was his – but that plan failed. David now sends a letter to the war where Uriah was fighting, telling the generals to put him on the front line where surely he would be killed in the war. David's attempt to cover up what he should have confessed led him further into chaos and confusion. But even in this, God never rejected or regretted David. How is it that God can regret Saul for simply not obeying His command but not reject David for all of the many things he has done just to cover up his own indiscretion?

The grace of God is not a system of qualifications but simply the will and plans of God, who is sovereign. Some may say that this even seems unfair of God but God is still sovereign and as stated during the anointing of David, God looks at the heart. We cannot adequately reason one over the other but we can prove that God has given us all a measure of grace and we must trust this with God's love towards us to not disqualify ourselves – not so much from our calling, but from our lives. Too often people fall prey to the pressure we incite with our own tendencies and give up on so much. Yes our calling suffers, but ultimately God desires for you to live, be well, whole, free, and abundant! That is God's heart toward us, and we must be mindful of that when we face similar temptations.

The agitation that comes with this anointing will never stop. Paul said;

For though I would desire to glory, I shall not be a fool; for I will say the truth: but now I forbear, lest any man should think of me above that which he seeth me to be, or that he heareth of me. And lest I should be exalted above

Marissa Farrow

measure through the abundance of the revelations, there was given to me a thorn in the flesh, the messenger of Satan to buffet me, lest I should be exalted above measure. For this thing I besought the Lord thrice, that it might depart from me. – II Corinthians 12:6-8 (KJV)

There are some thorns we may never be "delivered" from but we manage the thorns and the way it agitates you. There's a great weight that comes with the call and in many instances as here with Paul, these things come to keep us grounded. In this place, David was still a king – a great king – greatly called to lead and still wasn't removed from the desires of his flesh. It's impossible to expect to be prefect because you're called. Temptation is a weight that we must learn we can only bear in truth and honesty with God so that He can help us to maintain what we carry and what we feel. I am reminded often of the words of one of my favorite hymns:

Oh what peace we often forfeit, oh what needless pains we bear all because we do not carry everything to God in prayer. – Charles. C. Converse

The Amazing Weight   65

The weight of this agitation will come without much explanation. Don't beat yourself up over it and don't minimize your call because of it. But take it to God. David finds himself in a world of trouble that could have been avoided had he just ignored the desire to invite in this married woman. In the end, David wasn't cast out of his kingship nor the grace of God. After soul searching, David found himself in a place of repentance and God's grace stayed with him and followed him. Your failure doesn't have to equal your finale. It doesn't have to be the end of your life or your story. God's grace will find you if your heart is in the right place. God will help you bear the agitation and He will place people around you who can and will help you be accountable to your agitation. However, in everything seek Him only, as it is His desire to help you bear it. God's word reminds us:

Take my yoke upon you, and learn of me; for I am meek and lowly in heart: and ye shall find rest unto your souls. For my yoke is easy, and my burden is light. – Matthew 11:29-30 (KJV)

God gives us – with clear direction – the ways in which we can manage our yokes. That is by taking on His yoke and His burden, which is indicative of the fact that there will be burdens! However, the ones He allows us to experience are light because He knows how to help us handle it. The yoke is an instrument that was used during the agricultural climate of the scriptures. It was a wooden crosspiece that was fastened to the neck of two animals and the plow cart that they were pulling. The yoke was designed to bind the two together so that they wouldn't pull in different directions. It was uncomfortable, but necessary to position them for the job. Sometimes God has to put us in positions that are uncomfortable for the necessity of the will of God being fulfilled.

CHAPTER 6

The Demon of Depression

(Sometimes it's Just Too Much)

Depression is real. That's a pill many who make it to this chapter need to first digest. As I was preparing this reading, it was important for me to not be as political as I may have wanted to be but address the audience that will likely be reading this book. The church universal, the African American church as a subset of my immediate demographic reach. I find many who do not believe that faith and counseling belong in the same sentence. But the bible instructs us that "The fear of the Lord is the beginning of knowledge, but fools despise wisdom and instruction." – Proverbs 1:7 (NIV).

Wisdom: Wis·dom ['wizdəm/] - *the quality of having experience, knowledge, and good judgment; the quality of being wise.*

Wisdom, the bible speaks of wisdom. Good judgment; **the presence of counseling doesn't equal the absence of faith.** It simply means the presence of good judgment. When you know that you are carrying weights that you cannot handle, it is in the best of judgment to seek those who have the knowledge and practice of helping people who are under great pressure determine how to best compartmentalize all that they have to handle. Too often individuals suffer with the demon of depression and fail to acknowledge it. This disables them from obtaining the help that they desperately need, causing them to resort to measures that will often worsen their ailments by adding to their conditions. Depression is a spirit and there are individuals who are knowledgeable enough and equipped on how to handle people and situations plagued by depression.

As I write, I think about Pastor Andrew Stoecklein who recently ended his life after his battle with depression. A young vibrant thriving pastor with a beautiful wife and three young children who tragically took his own life due to depression. Let me preface this by saying I have no inside track to what his life was like, other than the public comment of his wife that he dealt with depression for quite some time. But even she didn't see this coming. It's possible to be struggling so silently that nobody around you can see that although you're successfully feeding others each week, you yourself lack the strength and support you need to battle your own fight. The question I'm drawn to is how could no one see this coming? His church? His staff? His wife? Do I blame them? No. Not at all. I'm saying that it's a scary thing when we can "perform" so well, when we can step up to the plate under the pressure of not letting others down so well, that nobody sees the warning signs of one who is about to bust under pressure. It speaks strongly to how well leaders and those who are called can stand broken, but if nobody stops to meet the needs and or lack of these leaders or give them the freedom without judgment to seek help for their hurt, we will continue to see this in church leadership. Counseling doesn't mean you are crazy or that you don't have enough faith to survive. It means you are wise enough to acknowledge your limitations as a human being and the needs you have to help you maintain the weight you carry.

Depression on the emotional end deals with severe despondency, or loss of hope. On the medical side, it could deal with the malfunction in the limbic system of the brain, which holds and control feelings and emotions. Depression can stem from something as simple as an emotional disposition or a medical one. It is important to never undermine people's emotions, even if you don't understand them.

Depression dates back to the bible, in that there were several central characters that we see deal experience depression. David was described as being troubled with deep despair in several of the psalms. When David lost his son because of his sin, he mourned for many days. But David's truthfulness with God shows us how we should come before God with our frailties so that He can help us bear them. "My guilt has overwhelmed me like a burden too heavy to bear" – Psalm 38:4 (KJV). Then we see David consistently trying to encourage himself and he raised this question to himself: "Why art thou case down, o my soul? And why art thou disquieted within me? Hope thou in God: for I shall yet praise him, who is the health of my countenance and my God." – Psalm 42:11 (KJV). David proves to us that extreme sadness and low spirits can even come upon the called, like a weight too heavy to bear. But our faith must be reflective of both honesty and wisdom. David isn't the only central character to deal with depression. If we look closely at the life of others such as Elijah who told the Lord, *I have had enough, he said. Take my life, I am not better than my ancestors."* – I Kings 19:4 (KJV). Elijah, a prophet of God, felt so weary he asked God to take his life. Jonah was so angry with God that he tried to run away. Job was so disturbed and distraught at the great devastation that God had allowed in his life. Job said, "I loathe my very life, therefore I will give free rein to my complaint and speak out in the bitterness of my soul." – Job 10:1 (KJV). Moses grieved because of the sin of people and we see the prophet Jeremiah, who dealt with loneliness, insecurities, and feelings of great defeat said, "Cursed be the day I was born... why did I ever come out of the womb to see trouble and sorrow and to end my days in shame." – Jeremiah 20:14, 18 (KJV). Many of the characters of the bible had a narrative at some point in their life about heavy or deep devastation or despondency. No where were we promised that our calling would protect us from ever feeling the anguish of life. But the lesson – and the common theme among all of these individuals – is that they **never let their weariness keep them from worship**. They maintained their worship for God and continued looking to God to help deliver them from the depth of devastation.

Today, we are blessed to have those who have received faith based training to help counsel, in addition to their secular licensing. Everyone needs someone to pour into or you will eventually collapse under the pressure of this great work. As honorable as it is, you need someone with whom you can share your deepest thoughts and realities. You cannot be so devoted to the people that you neglect yourself and become no good to yourself or anyone around you. Your mental well-being is just as much a requirement and necessity of this call as is your practices and study for perfecting it.

There's a great need for who you are, both to and in the kingdom of God. There's an even greater need for you to become all that God has ordained for your life and you can only do that when you stop trying to carry it all by yourself. There may be a great expectation from those you serve but there has to be an even greater awareness of what it takes to be effective in meeting their needs without compromising yours. If you believe that you are struggling with any level of depression or any other mentally challenging condition – especially if you are called and or in leadership, but certainly to those who are not – I admonish you today to not feel guilty for your desire to be holistically healthy.

CHAPTER 7

The Beautiful, Burdensome Call

(Let This Cup Pass from Me...Nevertheless)
Matthew 26

David is an extremely extraordinary character in the bible. I have found that much of David's life parallels to another man with a great calling, the man with the greatest name under the heavens and earth. Jesus Christ, savior of the world, redeemer of mankind. David was a man *after God's own heart* likely because he sought deeply to serve God and submitted himself despite his flaws. As we look at the life of Jesus, we see how he too carried and bore an amazing weight. The greatest man to ever walk the earth carried the weight of being in this world. During his 33 year tenure on earth, Jesus felt what it is we feel as he took on the form of human flesh and in that state, he felt the manifestation of emotions and feelings as we do.

In the beginning was the Word, and the Word was with God, and the Word was God.... The Word became flesh and made his dwelling among us. We have seen his glory, the glory of the one and only Son, who came from the Father, full of grace and truth. – John 1:1, 14 (NIV)

Jesus walked this earth and felt an array of things that gave Him a front row experience to what it is to carry an amazing weight. While His was far more divine than ours, Jesus experienced the pressures of a humanity that can often be viewed as cold, cruel, and even painful. Jesus had to deal with doubters, and non-believers. He had to deal with people who talked about him, and who called Him – as my mother used to say – "everything but a child of God." They accused him of not being who he said he was. They considered Him a sinner for not keeping the law as they thought it should be kept. Jesus had to deal with the emotional weariness of a mother losing her child, even on the cross. Can you imagine what it's like to know you have to fulfill this God-given assignment but the woman who birthed you is forced to watch you die a criminal's death? I can only imagine what it was like to see the weariness of your mother as she watched the wealth of your life be minimized to the blood draining from your side. Jesus carried much on His way to the cross. As much as He was 100% God, He was also 100% man. Jesus was able to maintain a divine disposition in a human experience because He was still God wrapped in flesh. But how beautiful is this call? To be the savior of the entire world. What an honor to not be a superhero but to be THE superhero? The one the entire world needed. But how burdensome a walk? To have to experience death by crucifixion with a journey that would carry you through being whipped, slapped, spat at, nailed, pierced and forced into the most physically anguishing death one could ever experience.

What a weight! What a weariness! What a moment! Weariness is inevitable in life. No matter how honorable the assignment. Jesus was sent to be savior to all of mankind, yet he felt weariness. If Jesus in hypostatic state being 100% God and 100% man can feel weariness, who are we to think we will escape the grips of weariness?

Jesus was aware of His assignment and the necessity of this call on His life of Messiah.

Messiah: mes·si·ah [/məˈsīə/]- the promised deliverer of the Jewish nation prophesied in the Hebrew Bible.

The call that is above any other call. Jesus, the name that is above any other name, experienced weariness in His walk with His father. This is biblically exhibited to us on more than one occasion – on His way to the cross and on the cross. Jesus is honored to be called. His disposition is reveled in scripture even at a young age. In Luke we find Jesus as a boy who has amazed the rabbinical scholars:

Now his parents went to Jerusalem every year at the feast of the Passover. And when he was twelve years old, they went up to Jerusalem after the custom of the feast. And when they had fulfilled the days, as they returned, the child Jesus tarried behind in Jerusalem; and Joseph and his mother knew not of it. But they, supposing him to have been in the company, went a day's journey; and they sought him among their kinsfolk and acquaintance.

And when they found him not, they turned back again to Jerusalem, seeking him. And it came to pass, that after three days they found him in the temple, sitting in the midst of the doctors, both hearing them, and asking them questions. And all that heard him were astonished at his understanding and answers. And when they saw him, they were amazed: and his mother said unto him, Son, why hast thou thus dealt with us? behold, thy father and I have sought thee sorrowing. And he said unto them, How is it that ye sought me? wist ye not that I must be about my Father's business? And they understood not the saying which he spake unto them. – Luke 2:41-50 (KJV)

Jesus knew from the early onset of His life that He was to be about His father's business and He wasn't discouraged in that. He understood His work and that it was completely inclusive of what His father sent Him to do. This call was one He believed in, as He was committed to fulfilling the calling. Many of us are truly honored to be called by God. It is something that you must appreciate with great deference because you understand that God can use anybody for whatever He wants. When calling announces itself in your life it is important to find honor in having been chosen by God to do anything for Him. The call is beautiful, honorable, and lovely because it's rare. Everyone is uniquely called by God, and uniquely gifted for their assignment. Every person is not called to reach everyone. There will be some lives and souls that only you and the uniqueness of your journey have the power to reach. When God graces you for an assignment, it is explicitly yours and sometimes that journey and the effectiveness of it is shaped in the processes you experience journeying into your call. That's what makes the calling beautiful, being first chosen, but then allowing God's infinite wisdom to shape your call into something that is uniquely yours and that uniquely qualifies you. God uses our experiences, and environments to grow us into individuals with understandings that give us unique ability to serve those we are called to.

Jesus had a beautiful call on His life. He was uniquely apart of God's plan to take a part of Himself from Himself, wrap Him in flesh, and send Him into the earth through a pure virgin to raise and nurture Him for the burden of the cross. Jesus is the promised Messiah. He healed the sick, raised the dead, fed the masses, and opened the ears of the deaf and the mouths of the muted – all while shutting the mouths of the doubters. He was aware of His assignment and the honor of it, yet when He came face to face with the reality of what He was preparing to face, Jesus utters from the garden of Gethsemane the words that have been a fundamental relief for Christians who face weariness to remind them that they're not by themselves, and it's ok to face it as long as they don't quit because of it. Jesus says, "...Father, if it be possible, let this cup pass from me: nevertheless not as I will, but as thou wilt." – Matthew 26:39 (KJV). This is the ultimate identification with humanity. Jesus feels the weariness of the calling ahead of him. The cross is before Him, betrayal is before Him, death is before Him, and Jesus understands the depths of what He is about to bear. In the amplified version of this scripture, it's worded: "My Father, if it is possible [that is, consistent with Your will], let this cup pass from Me; yet not as I will, but as You will." 'Let this cup pass from me' is Jesus identifying and making analogy of His call to the cross as a drink He doesn't want to take. It's the undertaking of something that if it were His choice He would have preferred not to do. This is one of the assurances we as believers have about the compassion of Christ. He doesn't expect us to always have preference towards carrying the weights we carry. That sometimes they are way too hard to bear. That in this moment, He too has felt what we have felt. If I don't have to go through with this, I prefer not to. Jesus gets it! As mundane as that may sound, Jesus understands and for anyone who has ever felt the weight of your calling was so heavy, you can rest assured you are not alone in this! You have a compassionate Christ who actually has experienced the weight. To take it further, not only does Jesus understand but He doesn't expect us to be perfect, He expects us to strive. But He doesn't disown those who run, those who are afraid, or those who are weary. He embraces us and empowers us to run on in the grace of His will.

Jesus is the perfect example of how we as humans can handle the presence of weariness and that which is burdensome. He expresses His desire. Father let this cup pass from me. But the victory is found in the resolve of His weariness of that burden. He says "Nevertheless, not my will but thy will be done." Jesus teaches us that the presence of weariness doesn't disqualify you from your assignment, but the way you handle it matters. He shows us that when you resolve yourself, what you do at the end of the day is what counts. If Jesus can feel weariness then we can feel weariness, but we must model ourselves after the way of Christ to embrace our assignment regardless of the burden that comes with it. Our call is not to ever feel the weight, our call is to be faithful no matter what the weight.

And being found in appearance as a man, he humbled himself by becoming obedient to death— even death on a cross! – Philippians 2:8 (NIV)

If it is our goal as believers to be Christ centered and Christ like, then we must follow the example of Christ to resolve our weariness to the victory of faith that is found in submitting yourself to the will of the Father. We must trust that God makes no mistakes and that His plans for us have no limit. Sometimes the weight we bear deals with loss and even death. But we can't limit our faith in God to only what He does with us in life, but also in death. God makes no error and His plans reign supreme over our feelings and our plans. Sometimes we won't understand why God makes us endure some of the difficult moments in our lives but we, like Christ, must learn to be faithful even when faith doesn't feel good. Faith isn't easy but with God we can bear that which He has beautifully and graciously given us that may be burdensome to us but necessary to Him, His plan, and His will. What I have realized is that we sometimes limit our faithfulness. But when we became believers we vowed to be unconditional in our faith. You cannot call it faith if it's conditional. Faith means no matter how heavy the weight I've been called to bear, I trust that the God who has called me to this will help me carry this until His will is made perfect in my life.

CHAPTER 8

Must Jesus Bear the Cross Alone?

(Suffering and Reigning With Christ)
II Timothy 2

Must Jesus bear the cross alone and all the world go free? No, there's a cross for everyone and there's a cross for me. – Thomas Shepherd

Words of a very powerful hymn, for we are all called to bear a cross. The understanding of this yields great relief to the fact that suffering with Christ is a part of this journey. What degree of suffering is that? Perhaps it's suffering persecution for simply being a Christian. Perhaps it's the kind of suffering that is endured in having to sacrifice fleshly wants for Godly will. But there will be some suffering. In II Timothy 2:12, we are reminded that there is reward to suffering, that "If we suffer, we shall also reign with him: if we deny him, he also will deny us"

(KJV). Suffer with Christ, reign with Christ. Deny Christ, be denied by Christ. The lesson here is that there is collateral for your consistency. The way you manage your ability to trust Christ, especially through suffering will reflect your level of faith in the plan of God. If Jesus was not void of suffering, why do we think we will be? Life here on earth wasn't designed to be a place that was so blissfully appealing that we wouldn't find more peace and solace in resting with God eternally than in this world. The pressures of this life comes with being in this world. A world that is full of trouble, envy, strife, malice, grief, racism, bigotry, misogyny, cynicism, selfishness and so many other things. But there's also much beauty in this life, beauty that was designed by God for us to enjoy but not to become so comfortable with this world. God's ultimate plan is that we live eternally with Him, and there is a collateral for being consistent with Christ. If we choose to be faithful to God in our trials, there is great reward. But if we choose to deny Christ in attempt to avoid suffering, we will be denied by Christ. *For what shall it profit a man, if he shall gain the whole world, and lose his own soul?* – Matthew 8:36 (KJV). What good is it if we enjoy the comforts of this life and lose the assurance our soul has for eternal life? The assurance we have is that the burden of suffering is not relative to just us. That everyone has a cross to bear – some seemingly heavier than others. They are all designed to introduce us to a God who sent a Son to share in our suffering that one day we may suffer no more.

We often bear the weight of feeling like we carry the weight by ourselves. But the truth is you are not alone and you never have been. Jesus endured the cross for us and the least we can do is be willing to endure for Him and for the cause of Christ that He may be glorified in our trials and suffering in His ability to keep us. Sometimes the suffering that we experience in life is not God's way of just allowing things to happen to us but sometimes we have to be broken in order for God to shape our spirits. Sometimes God has to tell us no to the things we may desire so that His will may always be accomplished. Suffering isn't limited to unwarranted suffering. In other cases, suffering can be the result of disobedience to God and this is what we as believers must learn to accept.

The Amazing Weight

While we serve a God who is compassionate and loving, there is a penalty for our disobedience and when we are defiant we cannot blame God for our suffering, no matter how much we repent and correct ourselves. Accept that there is a penalty to sin.

Suffering is a part of life and if we embrace that God exists in our suffering – either in plan or in purpose – we can lift some of the weight we bear when we experience suffering. Christ offers us a great resolve to it. We shall reign with Him. If we can maintain our faith through suffering, we shall one day reign with Christ. We must keep heaven and an eternal presence with God as our goal as Christians. Remember that the cares of this life are only temporary compared to the ultimate goal that is before us. If we can consistently remind ourselves that God is not just God in what we understand but even in that which we don't, we are able to set our faith in the fact that His ultimate plan for us will pay off through all of our suffering. Which brings us to the understanding that suffering is only temporary. Suffering is only a thing of this world. But this world isn't where we are destined to remain. This helps to develop the mentality that we can live with the trials we face in this place because they will not last forever. Pain, suffering, death, heartbreak, mortality, etc. This are all cares of this world.

Our day will be full of trouble. We must accept it. But like the Apostle Paul teaches us, "In everything give thanks. For this is the will of God in Christ Jesus concerning you." – I Thessalonians 5:18 (KJV). This is the position we must adopt in order to keep our minds focused on a perspective that helps us to properly place how to handle the cares of this life and who to look to. In everything, we should give thanks. But perhaps your question is how can I be thankful? Why should I be thankful? Well, simply because it's the will of the Father. As believers, we must learn to live with God's will for us being enough. Trusting the words found in Romans 8:28, where all things truly work together.

God's will for our lives supersede anything we can ever imagine for ourselves. And no, I won't say it's always easy to accept God's will but I will say we must question ourselves as believers when we resolve how we handle God's will. **It is possible to stand with God when you don't agree with God.** Sometimes you won't understand the manner of suffering, the reason for it, or the intensity of it. But can you trust God's sovereignty in it? It's our job as believers to simply trust. We may not understand, but we must trust; we may not get it, but we must trust it. We may not even want to go along with it but **like Christ, can you find yourself weary and still resolve to stick to your assignment?** Can you have hesitancy or even some resistance, but resolve yourself to still saying YES to the will of God under the belief that even the weariest of assignments in our lives have been thought out from end to beginning?

Remember the former things, those of long ago; I am God, and there is no other; I am God, and there is none like me. I make known the end from the beginning, from ancient times, what is still to come. I say, 'My purpose will stand, and I will do all that I please. – Isaiah 46:9-10

(NIV)

He is our God. The one who has seen and knows what was to come before it came. We may never understand Him, but can we trust Him? That's what it all boils down to. In fact, that is what religion is all about: faith. Faith that stands against anything. Faith in that which you cannot see but you can feel. If you trust Him enough to suffer with Him, there is a crown waiting for you to reign with Him eternally where there will be no more suffering.

Take suffering with stride and courage, knowing that it's all a part of the plan God has for you, which is perfect in the grand scheme of His will.

For I know the plans I have for you," declares the LORD, "plans to prosper you and not to harm you, plans to give you hope and a future. – Jeremiah 29:11 (NIV)

Have faith in the knowledge of God – found in His Word – that in the midst of any suffering we may endure there is an expected end that is glorious. That's how you learn to balance this Amazing Weight.

__Concluding Word__

See it through!

(You Are Necessary!)

From my spirit to yours...

This is my open letter to you. This is my heart for you, that you understand the necessity of your call. You are necessary and you are not by yourself. You are not the only person who has felt the struggle of bearing the weight. There is a great assignment that has been given solely to you. We have need of you! The kingdom at large, the kingdom of God. He hasn't given you this assignment without great consideration of your ability to see it through. But in order to walk into your place in God with the kind of power that helps you to bear this duality of feeling, you must actually walk in YOUR call. That which is given to you. David couldn't do his call like Saul did. He wasn't capable of fitting his garments. His armor was far too unfit and even heavier than what David was

Marissa Farrow   92

used to handling. Jesus couldn't skip His calling, or a world would have suffered. The people you are called to need you to be you! God makes no mistakes and you aren't here by incident nor accident. However, if you don't walk in your gift, you run the risk of carrying something that is essentially working against you. God can help you bear any burden you encounter, any weariness, any frustration, emotional unrest, hurt, grief, shame and more. But if you try to operate in a place that's not designed for you, you add to the load of that which you carry.

Sometimes the most difficult part of handling the weight is wondering if it's worth it. The answer is unequivocally YES! It is worth it because it all works within God's divine plan to bring humanity back to Himself. What good is it to live in His creation and not do the will of our Father? What reason would God have to just create us to have no purpose for putting us on this earth to go through this weight, just to end in nothing? There has to be faith in you to believe that God has something at the end of all of this that will make it all make sense.

You have not chosen Me, but I have chosen you and I have appointed and placed and purposefully planted you, so that you would go and bear fruit and keep on bearing, and that your fruit will remain and be lasting, ... – John 15:16 (AMP)

God didn't do this for the sake of having nothing to do. His goal from the beginning of creation after the fall of man was simply to repair humanity to Him. This is why He chose you! This is why the world has need of you in the place that God has ordained and designed your life to fill. Because He desires that we help to repair that which was broken when sin entered into the world. His Word tells us that we have been given the "Ministry of Reconciliation" (II Corinthians 5:18) and He chose us for it. Even before we had a chance to choose Him. That means that this great call was running after us before we had a chance to even see it coming. That is enough to qualify you despite your environment and other experiences that you may feel disqualify you. That's what gives you space and authority in the spirit realm even when you feel overwhelmed by life and all it brings; He called you! Often we feel like the things we experience disqualify us but most of the time those are the very things that make us humble for the call.

God chose the lowly things of this world and the despised things—and the things that are not—to nullify the things that are, so that no one may boast before him.
– I Corinthians 1:28-29 (NIV)

God chose the lowly things so that no one may boast before Him. Some of those weights or "thorns" even are designed to keep us grounded. They aren't there to be more than you can handle with the help of God. This is why you can never compare yourself to anyone else, or anything else other than the fact that we were chosen humbly, that we serve a God who has selected us from time to come into the earth and be used by Him. Comparison will kill. The ideas that others don't have as much to bear as you or that others have it easier than you will take your focus off of what you were called to manage and maintain.

You cannot accept your assignment and maintain what comes with your assignment if your focus is consistently built on what other people have in their hands. You must understand, appreciate, and walk in your calling in order to level off that which has already been given to you. Paul wrote to the church at Corinth and stated that:

... a great door and effectual is opened unto me, and there are many adversaries. – I Corinthians 16:9 (KJV)

Many adversaries – adversaries that are not limited to just being people. Whenever there is a great opportunity before you, adversaries can come in various forms. While often those adversaries come from external forces, we cannot forsake the notion that sometimes the adversary is the one we face within. Our own thoughts, challenges, and fears are the things we must fight through daily. Sometimes, our biggest weight can be the one we put on ourselves by trying to live up to the expectations of people, rather than obedience to God's will. Some of those adversaries cannot be avoided because they provide the effectiveness of your obedience and anointing.

The perspective we must have is that great opportunity is given to us to reach souls, change lives, and reconcile people back to God. Perhaps through the weight of your call, you haven't been able to see all that it is. Maybe you've compared yourself to your idea of "the called" but the called extends to all of us who have been given life. With life comes purpose and destiny. With this great opportunity before you, there will be great weight and at the end of the day, all I'm really saying is that "it's okay". You can manage it with God and He will help you bear what He's given you. God loves you and wants you to enjoy the blessings of that amazing gift He's placed within you. He wants you to see the beauty and honor in walking in your calling. God desires that we enjoy the blessing of the call. There's beauty in having been chosen by the God of the universe to be a part of His perfect plan! As much as we deal with the weight, we must develop and walk in the amazingness of it. You can handle the weight, you can handle the challenge, you can handle the process, you can handle the shaping, and you can handle the molding. You are built to stand under the pressure and to soar while carrying this *Amazing Weight*!

The Amazing Weight   97

36507511R10055

Made in the USA
Middletown, DE
17 February 2019